Woods and Chalices

Also by Tomaž Šalamun

The Selected Poems of Tomaž Šalamun

The Shepherd, the Hunter

The Four Questions of Melancholy:
New and Selected Poems

Feast

A Ballad for Metka Krašovec

Poker

Blackboards

The Book for My Brother

Tomaž Šalamun

Woods
and Chalices

Translated from the Slovenian
by Brian Henry and the author

HARCOURT, INC.

Orlando   Austin   New York   San Diego   London

Requests for permission to make copies of any part of the
work should be submitted online at www.harcourt.com/contact
or mailed to the following address: Permissions Department,
Houghton Mifflin Harcourt Publishing Company,
6277 Sea Harbor Drive, Orlando, Florida 32887-6777.

www.HarcourtBooks.com

This is a translation of *Gozd in kelihi*

First published in Slovenia by Cankarjeva zalozba, 2000

Publication acknowledgments appear on page 79 and
constitute a continuation of the copyright page.

Library of Congress Cataloging-in-Publication Data
Šalamun, Tomaž.
Woods and chalices / Tomaž Šalamun; translated from the Slovenian
by Brian Henry and the author.—1st U.S. ed.
p.   cm.
1. Šalamun, Tomaž—Translations into English.
I. Henry, Brian, 1972–   II. Title.
PG1919.29.A5.W66   2007
891.8'415—dc22   2007037468
ISBN 978-0-15-101425-5

Text set in Dante
Designed by Cathy Riggs

Printed in the United States of America
First U.S. edition
A C E G I K J H F D B

To Metka

CONTENTS

Woods and Chalices

THE LUCID SLOVENIAN GREEN

To step into the splash. To adorn oneself. I strode
the Karst valleys and bloomed. The underworld
is plastic and juicy. Whales dunk a little,
shoot a little. Chile is dewy, spring
is paper-wrapped. Girded like an ant,
like a cadet with argil. How do you reckon this? Bruised
like an icon? Blasted with small and large candles?
Slices are also in the trunk, there, where
squirrels and hornets fertilize tiny eggs. Caesar
walks staccato. Rome crawls by your feet. Wherever
the grape plucks, it starts to purl. The Irish saved Europe.
They piled sagas at fire sites. Everything northern
(Styria). There, in the forests, live char men
with flashing eyes. They snack on the *Book of Kells*.

MILLS

I grew up with eggplants. I stepped
from the truck, honey, chestnuts
rolled in honey. The higher, grayer part
creaked. It tottered. For a raven
that you snatch by the legs and spin like a bundle,
as long as it doesn't crash into a windowpane,
you don't know if it hits with its back or its eyes
closed, glued from fear. The windowpane
is not its beak. The raven has no beak.
The raven has only a sail with drawn-on
seed. Stars, ricocheting into the moon's
glass, go out. Between the time someone's
in the sky and the time he burns
in the sky is the beat of an eyelid. Water spins the logs.

IN THE TONGUES OF BELLS

I decant a blossom. It goes before you.
You're filled with Uriah. Green, tiny, and pressed.
Blueness is a furious cake, a round
cake where yearning sleeps. Are the balls
the balls of the earth? At wells
and fountains? At Atlas's pillar?
You say that you'd be my property.
You'd lose everything instantly.
I still wouldn't notice you anymore, injured.
I choose from the thickness. Honey collects
cries. And when the body thickens and you get up
because I dress you, because I congeal you.
I erase you back in the past. I draw
a white flap, shine a white flap.

THE CLOUDS OF TIEPOLO

The flock fell behind a hill. God
tottered. I chased a stall. Faded
and flew. When there's no syrup in the eyes, there's
no black man in the body. Virgo is in the loaf and creels.
She throws snowballs while standing. Plans unravel.
Clouds are rosy, as by Tiepolo.
As by Deacon and Aritreia. Tasso
kills a cricket. The knot spreads and advances
into the jacket with many *and*'s, as with the Danes,
who also translated the Bible like this. And so we have
and, and, and—no more—which the French
don't have. They have crouching planks there,
they call them elegance. The bridge goes in the eyes.
The soul in the railway. I puff, for I'm a pillar.

THE EDGE FROM WHERE WE MEASURE

Shiva gleams on a white pansy
and a penguin kicks the sphere. The radar
switches off. After speed? Nothing.
We only slept some twelve hours.
We were eating pizzas from Santa Fe
to Boston. Our minds sprinkled. The wheat
cleaved. I wanted to lick you on the neck.
What? Where? You rob the steering wheel
and the air. You stop. You smoke
and build a hut for little birds. Triangles,
you split open their feet, their toes
with the drawn-in bulbs for fingernails
which may be a football ground, a sea
or your screen. You inherited six of them.

FERRYMAN

I know you toil and loiter. The mourner
bids adieu. Her leaves' whiteness
recalls stalks. The graffiti of the poor
is under the earth. The adieu has staccato poses.
Drowns and flees. It resounds in the hut
when you wipe off the saddle. So we have
a wet ship and a dry rider. A worm
from a trunk and an outline from grain. The position
between the land and the river is wiped. The position
is wide. The river is cold. As long as he travels
parallel he doesn't need a draftsman.
But then, now will it whistle? Will there be
a bell, will it be perforated? Will the earth
split, as then within vineyards?

TIEPOLO AGAIN

The pill percolates. Methadone is technology.
Eyes in the Sava. There will be no more white tuck-ins.
Christ was exposed. Roe deer
kept their paws apart. Quilts
fluttered, and the wheat-like ones. We shelled
tweezers. Is there always skin under
the skin? Is the situation in the niches
and cockroaches and in the deep
Piranesi caves taken care of? Will lights be
by the legs? Will the dust burn? I gather myself
by Mormons. I embroider from lace, I have
a butterfly, Tasso, who drinks
from a bottle. Clouds rush like crumpled
wash, faster than watered guests.

IN THE TENT AMONG GRAPES

Don't sneak me onto mountains, chicken. Don't verify
your neighbor. You creep on my vaults. Where
paws and stars flash. Where Nietzsche
bites his knees (*Komarča!*) on the path above
Nice. What an azure milky whiteness!
Did you knead a little flour into torpedoes?
Did you sponsor a robbery of bees? Ears
adjust to the sky. Tendrils—if wholly
in white garlic—do you then tear them
like berries? We hear the engine, not the horse.
His eyes are poured out onto my hands.
Stumps and columns and stalks that you dunk
into the Mediterranean. Steve and Ken (asleep)
water flowers. The chimney branches out.

MOTHER AND DEATH

There is no grinding. Consumption is embittered.
The shove twists a white feather. The law
is in Kent's throat. White green violets.
The *schmeketa* pump is knocked down.
You revolt in the color of spilled wine.
You bring cakes and name them,
sell them here. White quails
have top-notch wings. The bone is among
the found. The found is expected
by witch doctors. Confirm to her what she saw.
Confirm to her that she was chatting.
That there are no remains. That the way is easy
always. That there is not even a drop
of reproach in front of the white mute.

ALONG GRAJENA RIVER

I helped
the peach
to braid itself.

Why did you already shut
your mouth on the mountain?
The sled

rolls,
turns round its axles.
It runs with

dogs and moose.
Boka is an ink stain.
Cut into the icy slope

and scattered powder.
The stone gives heat.
Ormož begs a hen.

I am Ban's daughter.
I played piano
in Poker,

the garden
did not keep.
Surely I must have died.

THE DEAD

Ou peut-être pas.
Perhaps their trumpets curve.
They forgot doorknobs in the floods
and now they dive for them.
Maybe they press the buttons
to rescind the aberrations.
Maybe they use crepe paper.
Maybe they're not so talentless
and crackle underwater like shells
and stones, such that every thousand years
of crackling harvests us
a tiny white stone.

ANCESTOR

Is it cold?
Are you snowed in?
The tent, does it still creak?

In a field near the Hrpelje-Kozina station
in the year 1911,
a cadet shot himself
in the mouth with a pistol.

Muldoon says Heaney is like the Vasa
ship. Built on three floors,
it was the world's biggest battleship.
It made half a mile
and capsized alone in a harbor.
The warriors are killed by insects
and lack of glycerine.
Scurvy corrodes their skulls.
Spruce trees shake off their seed and snow.
Between Zlatorog and the Savica waterfall
there is no hoarfrost.

ENAMEL

The tongue doesn't bind itself. It's a cleanser and a clean freak,
the marble-smooth skin of refined ladies,
a cork, a self-satisfied little clod.
When Alexander burns Persepolis, it can
meditate. It takes apart fighting lions
as if it's a silky little onion (diminutives strengthen,
they flood), their kindness is worse
than K's, who wishes us all well.
Am I a cold fish that kills Christ
with its tail? Saws through the cross? Should he fall
on his knees again, although he's still perforated
with nails? How will we do this, take him off
the cross so the knees will bend?
But what if they're already cold and stiff
like Cletus's corpse, whom Alexander undid
out of a guilty conscience, since he burned
Persepolis. Clearly Persepolis had to be
burned, the Rothschilds denationalized.

VASES

The sold-out butter rolls are padded.
Torcello burns. The khan who spat
over the drop is driving. The data is where

the woods shove. When we come through
the woods to the corpse, fond of air,
did we already see this hide?

Is it borrowed? Where are its signets
and crinolines and my stamps? *Die Gestalt,*
all scratched, cracked on the fork.

Or further inside. What do I know.
Did he ramble as in some kind of pot? We,
the types, must borrow a little stove. Atanor

wheezes. Cumin is brutally alive.
Waterlilies go through little needles. Dwarves
jump off. The does with snouts do not.

Frightened, they kneel on leaves. This lumberjack
appears in a porno. He's drenched.
He has an axe. The shirt fits him well.

The birdies accept him, and the elephants, marching
into the daylight, trod the reservoir alone.
The curtains only hindered them.

PESSOA SCOLDING WHITMAN

The whore of all solar systems and diligent
little ant, let's begin with this restriction. Until here,
cows, but here the guests can already wipe

their backs, except we dry this laundry
outdoors and the muffs also hang, although
it's summer at Jama in Bohinj. Špela is already

a great-grandmother now, she has a grandson
who plays hockey at Tufts, already forgotten as well,
like those who played chess here:

Cvit, Raša, Avčin, the awesome Montanists,
you can be Mister God in your country
(Raša), but here in Oxford we wear coats

differently, also stutter a little, out of pathos,
so this then pours into our Carinthian blood,
and after my sister, who got married

to Detela, bore a genius (deceased), and one
good and important writer,
now the living and the dead pull each other's hair

and with Barbara we're civil servants, telephones
constantly bang against us, and she was a little
in love, and I, too, and we sang

žure, put together for us by our mothers,
Madam Silva in her instance, and out
of this are born poets and civil servants,

who every free minute break for the Strand,
give search for Mikuž, another boy scout,
another nephew, another son, translating

that dreadful Latvian, I can find him
nowhere, and then Lojze arrives, the type
who would not believe I wished him well,

and yet today, first he gets lost in Harlem,
then he still comes up to Phillis,
who was wildly searching for him, and together

they watch *Microcosmos,* Phillis
howls with enthusiasm and they talk
fourteen hours without stopping, while

I, with Metka, rush to the same film:
how the snails fuck doesn't move us, hardly
staying upright against catatonic fits

of sleep because I must save my energy
so I will wake up in the morning because then
I furiously type and sniff everything: Barbara,

if Govic rises, I will stare once more
at the muscles of the inflated Avčin
rowing, how should I be interested in

the little sex lives of insects
and robbers, and whether I truly
forgot a gift for her birthday.

THE PACIFIC AGAIN

Open the bread.
Oil the wound.
Throw it up, puke it, speak it.
As long as you won't speak, it will hurt.
It will hurt, too, when you say it.
A caraway seed is a bath towel.
Chafers that fold on bones.
Puteshestveny's bundles are clearly starving.
The hunger reflects.
From the statue, from Oregon,
south of your Mihec, who is poured
by a lotus blossom emptying.
Order a mouth.
You don't know you can order it.
Few things are always technical.

LIBERO

The fan carried Liquido in his arms.
If I make him a face L will spring.
We also capitalize the countermand
and mythological monsters help us
so our apertures don't squirt.

Crown witness, crown garden,
watch the white lamb!

Boštjan read me and then
died underwater.

Ophelias on hooks, I'm a statue.
I'm a statue, fairy tales rustle.

Boštjan read me and then
died underwater.

Who will be the third Saint Sebastian?

The world wants to forget.
We want to forget
the dead and youth and freedom.

IN NEW YORK, AFTER DIPLOMATIC TRAINING

The good sides of a siege are not also those
smudged by a horse. There's a face
in the clause. Seven cherry trees. The notorious

seldom ever helps. He thinks mainly
about his blades. Do the smaller
and bushy help? Those seized below the deck?

The roots are to be followed to sand and sky.
The leaves rumble on them. If there's no balance
of silver and isotope—staffs—does it mean

we, too, can be happy? Without rocks,
there is no pier. The shelter extends to the bottom.
Objects are already sorted in the womb.

The creamy pigment sticks to some.
Someone will have swelled English,
a flayed stone in Potočka Zijalka. White dawn

that will suit him, dark green plastic
to pile up. Ribs creak
a bit on an uneven floor. You don't swing

your brain, you swing a dish. Once more you burn
crumbs, a face, pathos. You yellow
the black seed. I march nowhere. Honey flows

down my throat. Shed, breached, as if a machine gets dressed. Little barrels shielded us in the spirit of God's eye. We poured them out as we swam.

BOILING THROATS

With the screech owl the seed grows from the face.
The white vacuum pumps, the white vacuum pumps,
how you are squeezed. The cylinder is always strict.
The coil only sleeps in the clouds.
The cat and I, we scratch ourselves,
she will wreck my jacket.
She waits for fresh scales and the tone.
Clones evaporate faster.
At Fanelli's she whispers to herself the membrane
of the pigeon mail. She waits for fresh scales
and the tone. Little onion leaves are beneath the hooves
of fallen angels. They look like sacks.
They burst because of the farewell.
Anyone who goes soft gives away his voice.

THE CATALANS, THE MOORS

Poetry is a hatchery for martyrs. The river
rinses the butter. *Warum Nichts?* A window
is installed in a house, a house is installed in the dawn.
A clock strikes the quarter hour. I am left behind,
I am left behind, on the beach at Menorca
I expire like a crocodile. In the region
of Ciutat (with bicycle) near the young man
in his bathing suit from the twenties,
reading Cavafy. Did he have heavy hands?
Goran has heavy hands. I'm molasses,
don't forget that. Cat with cloudy
eyes. Voice found in the emptiness
and driving you to the precipice. Graveyards
as at Potočka Zijalka. Layers on layers.

SAND AND SPLEEN WERE LEFT IN YOUR NOSE

Blow into whales, schoolboy. The bait doesn't hurt.
Elephants, when alarmed, no longer know
the river. They carry penicillin between
ears and ribs, and trample reeds. Chess
comes from their backs. Birds' pecking
on a tarp is only one part of rocking. The sea
is black with fine sand. The white cork shines.
Palm trees that open beneath the robbed one
(all the checks, all the hash, two of Jure's letters),
you watch from two levels. The Ganges can wash
away the double. Luckily the current was fast enough
and in the morning, already at sunrise,
at the ritual murders, only one sipped and reaped
and didn't care at all to wake up.

ARM OUT AND POINT THE WAY

Vigorous, disfigured mice,
tassels or bonbons. Latte (the name
of the bitch with white fur), did the wheels

overeat like the heads of memory at the ends
of wood-limbs by Deacon? They were quite
devoured. Stretched out, softened,

given and given. Slime
washes windows. Peter, as a rule,
dances. Shoe shining is coming back,

the white matrix of the Announcing Angel.
People walking along roads
is coming back, the fluttering

of overcoats and the stopping of coaches.
The rushing to work and the paying
of tolls. We're a bunch of flowers. Napoleons

of the Bible. Worms between butter
and jam at the vaults of Inter Conti.
Ceelia Min signs.

The foam curses and counts.
A bottle is missing.
Surely it's hidden under the coverlet.

FALLOW LAND AND THE FATES

The boy scrubs the kitchen and crushes
the dot to mom. Godfathers' microwaves
catch fire. Snakes, Easter eggs, gray hats,
and crampon lamps flake from the pillars
on the walls. He who brews brandy
pants on screes, incantation.
Boils he who carries the mountain
and this one who unsaddles, supports yuppies.
I rotate breasts and papers. The river
makes the mesh. It's easy to find shapes
in the profiles of stones, but in the mud
there's the weight of the horse-collar. Sinking stools,
you can't pierce water! Only the scattered
water can drink water. The full water twists.

PERFECTION

Leather without history. Strength without
rickets. From a drawer. On the hand a wire. Blood
is silk. Walk silently. Blood is like
fruit. Here, too, is heated.
Shah's tanks are entrenched. First we thrashed
ourselves. We roared and got excited.
Mirrors have to function as ovens. You see them
from the road. On the machines producing
dreams. Some read between. The perfect
form springs up like an ear. I know
a chiropractor who can pull out your arm.
Five centimeters out of your shoulder.
Joints crunch. No need for oil. You spin
as you please. You leave when the tool falls asleep.

AVENUES

Invent a jacket for wearing out.
From a heap, a terrarium, little hairs.
From harnessed little ponies
and snorted snow.
Bitumen sits on stamps.
Whole corridors of sculpted
chewing gum underground.

Between seven and eight you can travel with a basket.
With a songbook, a flower bed, as you please.
You can dance with a puppet.
Silky hen, I stuff dollars into your mouth
to refresh the blood of your guitar.
We're happy
and we beam when we leave work.

DISLOCATED, CIRCULATING

Scrubbed hands, a goblet, a goblet,
a column and a dripped heart.
At the cross there's a stole and a signet, agave.
When sliding as on silk, white sheets
or linen, and a rotor flutters.
A mole sags under the soil.
He completes slits in the air.
Women yell, roll up arms,
does he make up for the fall of six million bison
over the cliffs of the Grand Canyon?
How many filaments are in the blood?
Or potato blossoms, blossoms
of pumpkins, blossoms of raspberries?
Organs shout down.
The cash box is iron.
Butterflies smack when they rise up in hope chests,
shoulder to shoulder, in the dark.
Did he slide?
Did grief produce juice?
Did he leave a trail like a snail,
only he went a little faster and not so
slowly?
Where was he intercepted?
Did they bury him without humus?
"Fast," he whispered.
"Brooklyn, this is the skin
cream."

CAR

The car is oily. Shutters in sleeves
rush. Trees crystallize, their juice
disputes the shutter. In history there are snails
and stepped-on snails. The dead and those
whose mouths we stretch. The juice costs.
The mower scores a salary. Can I catch
your tail and put you on the bus?
In big cities people don't walk
hunched. Yesterday I saw a cab driver
shot. On Third Avenue, at
Thirty-first Street. People interrupted
their reading. The young were worried. The police
were alert, as if they would train all night.
The air in the bus turned fresh.

ODESSA

You're lazy, Fedor, stupid and godfearing.
If you look at the bottom, you don't see crystals.
Crystals are bedsprings, they have noddles

in their robberies. As crooked as sea-
weed. It sways, sways and doesn't go down.
The water levels it. Crystals are mouths

of sweethearts. An agave is cut down with a hatchet, too.
A stomach, a sweetheart, an artichoke.
The neighbor's hand, clad in plastic,

cleaning up dog shit. We're in front
of Barnes & Noble. In front of the pyramids.
Across the street you can buy wine,

and when going to JFK and changing
at Howard Beach you watch
whales or sea elephants again (fish

that flash) for which the artist drew
gold pears, beards that reach
to the airborne planes and to the depths of the sea.

OFFSPRING AND THE BAPTISM

Canada begs one's butter. Everyone is in
the clearing. Godfather crouches, he's tender,
he tortures. The roost is mute. Iron-shod

I come. In the conical hayracks, in the intelligent
bull. Rustling massages the sky. The cellar
squats beneath itself. Seed undulates from the sphere.

Lamb's lightning utters the thought.
Sperm is behind the drawers, behind solace, love
is a red witness. We rented rivers

and channels and tunnels. We travel a little
stall in the wheat. I wet and splashed on you
on the raft as you daydreamed,

sheltered on the Ganges' smooth surface.
Did I come from lime? Did I make you
juice with murders? Glue myself to the little knitted

willow-made baskets? When the basket
gently banged, language slipped
and sizzled. It leaped over fields. The water

was yellow, brown, downtrodden. The language
frayed. Does the bloom evolve? Mountains
drop into butter. A new fist

picks them up. It makes plants from rice. The snow
jumps at and batters the fields. If I didn't
protect your mouth, the cross would rot.

WASHINGTON

No one rides on
the crest. No one stops Rembrandt.
Trousers worn down on parmesan.
On the crests of the hooved.

Dinosaurs are made of rubber,
more precisely, of green
water-soluble chewing
gum and that molasses

à la watered-down sherry.
You are drunk.
Of course I reserved two beds.
Of course I will force the door, what do I care.

THE KING LIKES THE SUN

Few of the ones he granted requested
the invention. He didn't overlook it.
He wasn't able to overlook it.
It opens like a patch. The empire
condenses and softens. First
there are calluses. Then the wrap
goes numb. The smell of pavement starts
to boil. The pole obtains azure,
water's dark surface. Someone from afar
leaps, as an animal would fall
from a roof. He uses his arms to seize.
The pole bends. Icicles
sizzle in the sun, are noted.
The little bird pecked up the nest.

YOU ARE AT HOME HERE

I study lungs. I go nowhere.
I gaze at the edge of white mountains. I want to die.
The path goes into money. Now I can occupy a calendar
of authority and give away the tent. They are twisted
into the song, the food, the sea. They are dressed
in white stories. He wasn't hoarse, who didn't know,
a stamp healed the window and the wound together.
The motive is beautiful. The elephant is bottomless.
It spins vases and the girls in them.
It spills itself on little cups, a coffee, an airplane
kneels in the overgrown grass. This isn't my bread.
The bread is all yours. It adorns itself with claws.
Jump into the factory of rough flags
and stretch the edge. Fall asleep with the stretched edge.

BITES AND HAPPINESS

These are the little ribs of my patrons.
They tramp in the black residue. They stir
loam shipward, oust birds from *v*'s and *c*'s.
There are vast white plains seen
only by gargoyles. The sun
doesn't lessen the animals' luster. Gnats move
with the raft on the river. Thorns cannot help
themselves with water. You retreat with the drums,
Tugo. You space out wedges and cotton wads,
forget about blunt blows and cathedral bones.
The entire temple seethes. Dwarves with lanterns
don't depict even the first ring. Between
the dug-in hoof and the earth (graves of young
potentates) there's not enough sturdy concentration.

BARUZZA

Vendramin! Sharpen it! I tell you
to sharpen it but not so ardently
that you break it again.

You cleaned your shoes with your shawl,
what is this, Vendramin, the mediation
between Verdurin and the Misses Nardelli?

Both nailed dogs onto placards.
Take an eraser, a lamp, and a huge
hammer, they barely lifted it.

The nailing was done by servants.
The lifting was done by servants, too.
And in the time when there were no

big billboards yet, they observed
the clear seabed at Silba.
There, where Azra coated you

with tar. Opened your throat,
spread it toward the sun,
as Isis to me, Anubis.

THE LINDEN TREE

You didn't satisfy *to us,* man from Australia,
in the magnetic field you acted like a she-kale.
Cuba squeezes out the blue snake. We hugged you.

A flash of lightning reports on heaven and spills Fatima.
Remember the asphalt for the million believers.
Remember that on those small gardens, among

ocean 'shrooms and the nation similar
to Slovenians—similarly suppressed, only that
they had three more rags in history (half the world)—

murmuring between Tomar and Fatima,
between the ordained fourth miracle and the piece
of cheese, happens. Did you see how the crowd's voice

strengthened? Did you feel what the feminine principle is
(Mary) and how in Tomar (painted incessantly by Marko
Jakše, although he was never there) the hall

stirs, stirs centuries, and lifts freemasons
like some sort of dwarf. Dwarves
today just wrap ribs to pigeons.

And the pigeon (with the brush), another pigeon
(like wurst, in salted and cloudy paper,
feasting), Bob Perelman is the pigeon.

He comes (twenty-five years after
he drew his blood-tax in Arena), a quarter
of a century I guarded him like my own blind

beaver who will blast into the dark
corridors of America with the one
small, tram-like shift. *To us* instead of *us*.

doctorate man! fucking
otter: *recommended reading*
fucking on beaches, on damp grass
fucking with universal doctrines: labor
fucking with steamships, in the clouds
fucking in the arena with moby dick, fucking with partisans
smog: hoarfrost
fucking on the cliffs of dubrovnik, the patriot
fucking with contessa adriana gardi bondi
she disappeared and returned with a towel
heard the awful splash and frodo yelling: auuuu!
fucking with the tatra mountains, with white wine
with radio antennae, I live off lights
I live off ljubljana's liberation M.S., the signet!
imprimatur: fucking with chains stacked on cushions
the sun: corinthus
fucking under right angles, with fields
with the fast-turning cloud, with cinema
fucking with the colossal apparatus: bled
hey, hey, how are you? I hope you're fine
I hope you're well, welcome!
bohinj: fucking with aspirin
baltimore: delegates
barcaiolo sul mare, fucking with buveurs d'ames
that cathy barbarian would sing *black is the color,* fucking
the cat, the wolf, pasha who rides an elephant
that we'd drink wine, bread, indulge in grass around the house

se i languidi miei sguardi, enjoy boris's first-class certificate
with fucking how, with tea at five
with regular life, with the pleasure of company and travels
with this that I wouldn't let wicked people across the threshold
    of my home
because I stood up in solitude, because the sun bathed me
I'd gladly die mute, friend
pure as the oak

WE LIVED IN A HUT, SHIVERING WITH COLD

Is the little bird torn apart
by a paw? Lights switch on, at least
one juxtaposition between

tree
trunks. On handcarts
(wheelbarrows) there are

blue baby
bags. An unguaranteed
growth ring is left

on the asphalt.
The gadget with which
you fatten

your ears,
rubbed out from sky-
lights. The other

will understand all of this
when he takes the time.
The Danube will open its graves.

AT LOW TIDE . . .

At low tide the footprints are blue
and I long for the sinkhole.

Show me what you wrote.
My poems are genitalia.

BLUE WAVE

Where you offer your fuck-crazed mood,
I'm already relieved. Mantras
are morbidized. They recoiled
in loops on the racks, reflected
the mouth and voice of Prince Bolkonski.
I eat from the flock. You contributed
nothing to this. You gave
and then burnished. Algae turned up
beneath the backstay. You broke the incision.
You devour the fairy tale with an angle.
Like those weary *menefreghisti* that eat their fill
of the sun and fall asleep
on a wave. It's hard to move
the solar system off the retina this way.

COLOMBIA

Cats have set themselves on wings.
Buttons have buttercups. Hares are soft meat,
hares are soft meat, they quiver and throng.
They rise the sun, actually hold it
on little poles planted in the sand.
Water fortifies the poles in river sand. A pool
vibrates differently from clay. It spills itself
and does not come back rhythmically. The sea
is a guarantee and the nosy are full of adrenaline.
And now? How are you? Is there also a membrane
in the volcano along which the tongue glides?
That which stirs the cells of memory
and undulates the body and screams
when the sun soaks, soaks, roasting in Iška?

AND ON THE SLOPES OF LA PAZ

Bushels full of little lymphs.
Paper caps of endless yarn.
There are no more yards, Thursdays,

orphans released in rows of four,
blind men playing the accordion
beneath the chestnuts or at the corner

of Langus and Jama.
Only flagellates yearn
and die with comforted,

lamenting lungs. Where are
the trash bags I smashed
on the heads of maids and their

officers, so that white Jules Verne
balloons kept escaping from them
on footpaths in the park, like those

found these days only in Persia.
In Shiraz young men grow out of Cretan
vases. In Knossos they are showy,

because there's no more dust and macadam
and stockings anymore. Are you falling? In Lisbon,
at Alfama, you ignite the birds, and in Trieste,

in the park of Villa Rossetti,
there are black turtle bellies and fathers
who portray themselves as goldfish.

COAT OF ARMS

The wet sun stands on dark bricks.
Through the king's mouth we see teeth.
He sews lips. The owl moves its head.
She's tired, drowsy, and black.
She doesn't glow in gold like she'd have to.

FIERY CHARIOT

The bull's berry walks on wires.
The windowpanes are wounds.
They hiss when the jet streams from the silver
kettle and a giant flings a discus.
It turns its head. The helmet touches the tip.

SHIFTING THE DEDICATIONS

The juice is sore. The stupor endures the bag. When you hurry,
you stand up, smith yourself. The vault is still coming.
You believe, you believe, you believe in your fruit.
Exhausted, cruel, and lazy, do your eyebrows blaze
with your loot? What else do you still know, incised one?
You mellow from sores and pains, no longer mine.
You bound yourself to nothing. Are you betraying me
to awaken me? So I would squeal and hurt?
You drown in your huge shoes, soldier,
naked to the waist, drawn by the manuscript.
One could hardly see water under the thick green
August leaves and the flickering of the centurion.
You rolled, as a priest would sneakily count
handfuls of earth. The sun was worn out.

WASHING IN GOLD

Dakinis dig and plow and babble
and push shingles off the roof.
The clod is microtone.
The pane shakes against the steamship.

Isaac Luria wasn't for food.
He was for strong ingredients
in an obscure diet
like hair, bonbons.
He smelled sweet and emptied himself, hugged.
He stooped under the water because he sang.

Brahmins came for the signet.
Roe deer drank off layers of water.
Crickets still had extra buckets
on their backs, they poured themselves.

Sometimes, an entire bucket would roll off
a clumsy cricket, with the sponge.
Before, the sponge swam in the water in the bucket
on the cricket's back under the water.

Light and light do not touch.
The belly of God is between, totally stuffed.
He barely breathes and unfolds.
Sometimes a butterfly's wing tickles him
when he starts to eat his own pupa.

THE WOOD'S WHITE ARM

You don't have the right to eat even the filly
of the little paw. Nathan's headboard is in Prague.
God knows if he sleeps peacefully. The little paw
wears out and drinks by the stone. The will flies around
the birch. The firewood is weak from waiting.
Are the green birds already throwing up at Komna?
To want and wish to follow into a duvet.
Push-ups are done there. Towns are built
there and shells are sought, the handcarts
in the mines prepare. Did I comfort
you then? Do you still wonder,
when did I comfort you? There were needles
all around and a spruce and soft moss
and as now: spring was announcing itself.

THE KID FROM HARKOV

Strips of thin plate tissue are love
without a cell. Snails gush saliva
and toads. They glaze a cotton wad
for the orthodox church growing on
white sand and from bones. Madam
Yaremenko says there was no right
tone. She missed the czarist gestures
from Bijela Crkva. Katarina liked
Onjegin and Ivan the Terrible lions.
Karadjordjevičes killed the Cincars.
The Hellenes lasted on vases.
I reached with a hand under the napkins.
There was straw, and here and there some
gefilte fish. Send me the recipe for borscht.

PORTA DI LEONE

Sand and rollerblades and a tailor,
he keeps bedsprings in the pigment and the mouth.
It seems he thwarted the upholsterer.
Do you keep flour, too? Do any flowers fall
on its head? In the narrow streets they're tall.
What if a gas pump hit someone
walking the street? He didn't walk. He didn't
walk, it just happened this way, what if
it didn't happen? Little donkeys
keep coming back. They bray before evening.
The door opens, the dung doesn't disturb.
Frogs approach Porta di Leone
and we quelled the mosquito with poplars.
They grew up under Mussolini.

PALEOCHORA

Ron's land is veiled by a padlock.
Men are on guns.
Time doesn't have a dark suit anymore,

cows have stovepipes in their stomachs.
Multiplied, they give a cleaver.
A white meadow, white millet,

white millet for brother horses.
I snacked on a strap.
The cave got larger.

The blueness didn't start to tremble only around
birds, the bird itself turned
blue, constituent.

He invented a typewriter
on a vacuum, a tunnel in a cave
that failed. Bill Gates

sealed off his ear. The hut
changes into fear. Fear
opens itself into the dark slippage of cards.

I wanted to oblige my friend
so he could play bridge.
The pea, too, is a miracle of the Trinity.

PERSIA

Hey, monarch, ferry me across
the river. A nettle nips, a nettle
does not nip, a nettle

does not die from frost. We gurgle
tar, still unborn
piglet with pretty and white and long

hair, else
sorrow, sores, pain,
and vertigo.

Do you also fight for her like a lion?
For screams I'm patriotic.
Sidewalks are kind.

The corners of sidewalks are kind
to invalids. To return love to the blind.
To make it dewy, to make it

seen, to make it watered
by their gazes. To return sight to the blind.
I will thrust the smell of river sand.

Parafilled little wretch on a morbid plank.
Bronze radiates. It pours from leaves and creaks,
rends grease. *Phantasia kataleptikè?*
Rabbits, snow, bushes, boots leak,
I lie unconscious by the river. Outer space
gulped dumplings. The smell was constant.
Inside we stored pieces of gold and wiped,
wiped river stones. *Is it worth*
tipping? Certainly. Then where is
the sail that cleans the gazelle's leap? We leap
through soot. Through flaming hoops,
twice. The animals' skin crumbles in the cinema.
The slippery surface turns and changes.
The podium creaks. The road is fresh and aches.

OLIVE TREES

The act is luminous. Out of wire, out of
sage, out of gray green puffs of air.
I dreamed Poof had brambles instead of
fur. The foam had patience.
Did you find a chanterelle? With every layer
of night a little coat is pulled on.
The word made the river and the waterfall
and the power plant and the mill. The Mitchourins
already to the Mesopotamians. They rolled
rocks in front of a town gate. They stood
on a hoop. The space between the word
and heralds (the shoes pinched) was changed
by the view. By the pressure on the skin
of olive trees' drums starting to ski on the wilderness.

MORNINGS

The poem shines the saw. I don't know it
by heart. The spit is merry and embraced,
soaked with bast. The white one wants, the dowry
wants, you climb and hurtle on spikes.
In front of Agnes Martin's canvas (Pace
Wildenstein) I came across two
dervishes. They were Turks. They had
hair combed like a black apple.
Are white caps humble?
Isn't the strike the sun brings on beams
(laid down with force) too dangerous?
I kiss the earth. Deepen the air
and dust. I shift gears
and stand up. Lapis lazuli blots me.

IT BLUNTS

Only protosynaptic measures have blackened
God's blueness. Nightmare is balsam sleep.
Rivers smell fragrant, the gallows. I'm worth the brow.
Weary and wooden. How are the legs?
Some say they're real.

Will he snatch a bigger slice of bread of God's love?

MARASCA

The sour cherry is a steamship's body.
Panta rei sleeps.

SCARLET TOGA

Overnight snowfall filled everything.
The pools are emeralds.
I talked to people
with noble mouths.

They brought cymbals and bronze,
a chafer wrapped in stiff paper,
they swung it in a handcart and sang,
we heard how the fortresses were knocked down.
The dust from the ruins is still damp.

We burned down and built from
the shit of camels and cows.
Yesterday on Elizabeth Street I saw
a man who had such a hat.

At Starbucks it truly smells
of the roasteries of Trieste, the aroma
they first carried away to Seattle.
We were still talking about two

supermodels (about cow dung),
hairstyles, little braids, goggles,
about the carefully outworn,
and I injected into myself
this text into the photo:

Jorge Vegas, soft shadow friend
whisper fire. Caress the blood
within. Set free the buddha
cat in me, into ginger
haven, sugar stone smile . . .

SHEPHERD, YOU ARE JUST LEARNING

Penetrate, don't outwit. One iota,
two people's houses. Laughlin. I'm blotting.
From everything wrecked, white gray glances.
The little mill didn't spin. It was all about a heavy
paw. It's purified. Forged by faith and poured.
The little coat is not rickety. It's cast in a green
and silver building. If you break into a chafer's belly
with your head, the water comes springing. *Torna,*
which propel hard drives, are from garlic.
As if I'd have more iron inside my palm.
Water is always young, excluded, and self-
pleased. Ken Jacobs arranged the red plateau
on which Norse was written, burning
on Chambers Street. Egypt cut itself.

THE CUBE THAT SPINS AND SIZZLES,
CIRCUMSCRIBES THE CIRCLE

Noble little grain, farina,
dark edge of gold icons,
it rolls.

Is the bell mucus, the blackboard stored
with the petition flower?

Mormons have all the names in the gullet.
But with me the watch is warm, boy-scout-like.

Jure Detela was an athlete.
All night we sat on the bench in Zvezda Park,
I guarded him and convinced him
not to go and clip the bears' fence.
This was wrestling with an angel.

His eyes poured out of him. It was rustling
when the morning rose.

He was comforted, fed,
and willing.
Beheaded.

As if he did clip the fence.

THE MAN I RESPECTED

When I returned from Mexico, I looked like
death. My mouth collapsed
and disintegrated. I was paying a penalty
for my sins, my palate had dissolved.
I could touch my brain with my tongue.
It was painful, horrible, and sweet.
While Svetozar sat outside in the waiting room,
I tore down the instrument case.
No, I am not being precise: he left the office
before me, I only suspected who he was, I didn't even
know him. When I sat in the chair,
my energy tore down the instrument case.
To pass from world to world
means an earthquake. Yesterday he died.

THE HIDDEN WHEEL OF CATHERINE OF SIENA

How does the butler configure?
He eats out of a hand. He strokes his nickname,
the number six. The beak is rasped,

sawdust whistles under right angles. It's yellow
where it isn't cut through. Softly,
we could stuff daisies into it, and as with hair

and fingernails, there is no pain.
The pain is in the missing part.
In the missing part the impaled daisy

flutters. Is the butler
then a Venetian mask? Clarissas,
pacing solemnly between the power plant

and the grilles in Siena.
In Assisi. I was steered into the wheel.
And when I, drowsy on the piazza,

thought of Pincherle, nibbled
gelati and *fave* and massaged
my heart, I realized

the nave is empty. There are no side
naves. There is no roof. Between the sky
and the pavement there is not even a tiny circle.

WHITE CONES

Vanilla, the ruin, house of silence, threads.
The starling stipples the sky and knocks down granite.
It eats stars. Small, dirty boxes
full of worms. Meccas flap.
Dervishes are thimbles on neighbors.
In the hall there's a dome. In the dome
there are boxsprings overturned.
I.e., turned voraciously.

HORSES AND MILLET

The mind has no swings.
It's wacky, frozen in lianas.
When they gash, they're like doorknobs.
The flame in them burns.
The worms get a tarp on their eyes,
cows eat the millet on the tarp,
not shrubs.

The louse creeps into them and falls asleep.

HENRY OF TOULOUSE, IS THAT YOU?

What did we fly over?
Which boxes did we fly over?
Which yellow boxes did we fly over?
Vases pull lightbulbs from their mouths, shine in white.

The clause is pressed into the gums.
Hats cover only undisciplined mice,
the opposite of what we'd expect.
The axis is unavoidable.

Is that you, caraway seed?
What did we fly over?

NEW YORK–MONTREAL TRAIN,
24 JANUARY, 1974

At first I was shaking like a switch in water
because of "the chain of accidents." My second thought
was that I'd gladly be as systematic

as Swedenborg was. Was the frame clear
and did I accept it, though all the zones
of my body had yet to go through the slot? Immediately after—

I saw it in a flash—angels are censorship
and fog, merely a field of space that hauls you
toward the center. They quickly paled and glued

in a lump. I felt physical hands,
they caught me gently under the armpits. The air
whirred, but not as if the firm body

would go through, it was as if someone were dragging me
through milk. They all expected me, though
they noticed my physical presence only

gradually: first the old, then the middle-aged,
then the young. As if someone with a rheostat
had broadened their field of vision.

Some reported (let me know)
that they were carrots, and that their scraped
skin was already in the earth. Some felt clearly

that they must go only headfirst through
the waterfall. I was interested, they were here
by some selection, but this thought died away because

they stopped it and I couldn't utter it.
It was like stopping a drop that falls
into water and then spreads in circles.

Clear waves, I traveled with them.
A solid lump (above my head)
licked and flooded me with pity

and delight. A strand (a cone) coming from
this lump pulled me apart,
spread me horizontally, though I was the same.

I knew: they have other sources, infinitely
more powerful, infinitely more tranquil.
I noticed an apparent affinity in dress.

Veils (clouds) at the height of the chest. I didn't walk
along the ground, but along something hanged, resembling
ice or glass (optically), though I felt it all:

the moss, the parquet, the grass, the asphalt (green!).
I didn't see this with eyes but with skin,
as if the skin were watching. At the same time I read Haiku,

I. G. Plamen, and for some time *The Village Voice.*
I was in the train and looking through the window, reading
    again.
In an instant I grasped everything. Language is "articulated"
    and "mute"

at the same time, it occurs in tepid flashes. Accidents
are the humus. As if ping-pong balls would fly
in all directions at once and massage you.

THE WEST

There's no Kowalski in a cookie, in the dark there's only
le sucre. The measure, gray little measure, three.
I box the fruit to burst the fruit. The gush

is in the wretch. The moon is in the extinct. Tiny frogs
are seamstresses, they unstitch. Does grief shout in the valley?
Does it rebound off radiators? Indians

who rebound from the countryside with candlesticks
and a pickaxe. You fall on Belarus and turn
in the seaweed. A stain, like patchwork, leaves,

gathering by naked trunks. Exceptionally
with blinkers. Exceptionally with a hand, exceptionally
with a foot, sails cross themselves.

A salmon rushes toward semen. Does it spit out
a bomb and the river and the earth?
Not everyone is planed behind the house. It's important,

what the entrance to the underworld is like.
If toadstools faded. He tugged his arm inward.
He lowered his altitude. He fell from a horse

long ago. Needles are on the ground again, where
yesterday was a cherry tree. In Bavaria
they learned how to throw the mortar. To make it

radiant when it drops from the house.
Eyes, a spirit taken on a plate, the fever calms.
You climb because you need solitude.

You need solitude because of the edge.
In the cellar there are little birds shifting from leg
to leg. You burn only Roman buildings.

I hurled myself onto cushions. First we hugged,
then kissed, then stripped,
then dressed. I wouldn't allow it. I wouldn't

shut him in the lens. We only held hands
like two little girls. He boils
monkeys, he strained himself, too.

Leaves had not started to fall. It's cheaper
if they move him. At the same time he's filled with flour
and sand and I don't know how to read signals.

PUBLICATION ACKNOWLEDGMENTS

Grateful acknowledgment is made to the following publications, in which these poems first appeared: *Blackbird:* "Ancestor," "Colombia," "Marasca," "Perfection," "Washington"; *Black Warrior Review:* "The Hidden Wheel of Catherine of Siena"; *Boston Review:* "You Are at Home Here"; *Circumference:* "New York–Montreal Train, 24 January, 1974"; *Conjunctions:* "Arm Out and Point the Way," "The Linden Tree," "Pessoa Scolding Whitman"; *Crazyhorse:* "Mother and Death"; *Cutbank:* "Along Grajena River," "At low tide . . . ," "Baruzza," "Blue Wave," "Fallow Land and the Fates"; *Denver Quarterly:* "The King Likes the Sun"; *Fence:* "Olive Trees"; *Field:* "Offspring and the Baptism"; *Gulf Coast:* "The Catalans, the Moors," "The Dead"; *Jacket:* "Coat of Arms," "Fiery Chariot"; *The Modern Review* (Canada): "The Kid from Harkov," "Mills," "Paleochora," "Washing in Gold"; *New Ohio Review:* "Porta di Leone," "Vases"; *North American Review:* "And on the Slopes of La Paz"; *The New Republic:* "Persia"; *Octopus:* "In the Tongues of Bells," "The Lucid Slovenian Green"; *The Paris Review:* "We Lived in a Hut, Shivering with Cold"; *Poetry Review* (UK): "The Man I Respected," "Scarlet Toga"; *Subtropics:* "Boiling Throats"; *turnrow:* "The West."

All poems were translated by Brian Henry and the author, except "Academy of American Poets," "Ancestor," "At low tide . . . ," "Car," "The Catalans, the Moors," "Coat of Arms," "Colombia,"

"Fiery Chariot," "Holy Science," "The Man I Respected," "New York–Montreal Train, 24 January, 1974," "Persia," "Pessoa Scolding Whitman," "Scarlet Toga," "Washing in Gold," "Washington," and "You Are at Home Here," which were translated by Brian Henry.

ABOUT THE TRANSLATOR

Brian Henry has published five books of poetry, including *Quarantine* (nominated for the National Book Award and the Pulitzer Prize), *The Stripping Point*, and *Astronaut*, which also appeared in Slovenian. He has co-edited *Verse* magazine since 1995. He reviews poetry for the *New York Times Book Review*, the *Times Literary Supplement*, the *Boston Review*, *Jacket*, and other publications. He teaches at the University of Richmond in Virginia.